Happy Re

Blessings on your head!

Life is good!

Gayle

Baloney Slice Theology

December 2002

To Deb ~

Within a circle of grace,
may we always know how
easily bread and water
can be toast and tea.

♥Candy Wasser

Baloney Slice Theology

Sandwiching the Baloney of Everyday Existence
Between
Thick Slices of The Bread of Life

Gayle Norris

This is dedicated to my husband Steve
who always sees me as better than I really am,

To my children Jennifer and Stephanie
who are individually poles apart from me
yet mirror me so much

And to my friends and family
because of all we share.

I am blessed through each of you.

Introduction

Oswald Chambers said, "We look for visions of heaven and we never dream that all the time God is in the commonplace things and people around us." Jesus noticed the common things...lilies of the field[1]...sparrows that fall[2]...hairs of your head[3]...sheep[4].... He spoke to people about those things because they were familiar. Life is full of not-so-glorious, mundane, boring stuff. Some people call it baloney. Whatever you call it, the trick is to slap it between thick slices of the Bread of Life.[5]

You know the old saying: "It's Greek to me." Well, I don't have a Greek translation, but the Bible does sometimes seem foreign. When I find something in it that speaks to me, I haul it around and rub up against it. Eventually, like the toy rabbit that gets to be real through much loving in <u>The Velveteen Rabbit</u>,[6] special verses come alive to me.

When David[7] says, "Thy word have I hid in my heart..." that's what he's talking about: embracing God's word till it becomes genuinely part of us. Ordinary existence gets sandwiched in the Bread of Life...

We do not dwell in obscurity as long as we realize God is in the most ordinary with us. Perhaps the foolishness of God[8] is a big part of Christianity. So, forgive my foolishness as I share with you my spiritual lunch...

Baloney Slice Theology!

---

[1] Luke 12:27

[2] Matthew 10:29

[3] Matthew 10:30

[4] Luke 15:4

[5] John 6:35

[6] The children's book by Margery Williams

[7] Psalms 119:11

[8] 1st Corinthians 1:25

Contents

Dust

If

You

Must ...

Dust Bunnies

God gave us a gene for almost everything: the color of your eyes and hair, size of your nose and length of your toes. I believe there is also a Housekeeping Gene.

Grandmother was strong evidence of its existence. Her house was immaculate. Mother inherited the Housekeeping Gene. When I was small, a neighbor lady told me that our house was cleaner before Mother started cleaning than her own was when she finished. This phenomenon was not due to any help from me...

As a child I slept much better at night
Knowing dust bunnies lived under my bed
Because if any monsters came,
The bunnies thumped them on the head.

I hated it when Mother mopped
And shooed my dust bunnies away,
So I'd hide the big ones under my pillow
And keep them anyway.

I let them loose as soon as I could
So they would not smother.
They protected me from monsters:
I protected them from Mother.

Luke 10

My husband did inherit the dominant Housekeeping Gene. He does not believe dust bunnies are endangered species. We were married five years before he left his first dirty sock on the floor. I stepped out of the shower one day and there it was, just lying there: cotton confirmation that he really was human.

I was so excited, I just ran through the house waving that sock over my head. I hollered to the girls that daddy left a sock on the floor. It was a mistake on my part, because their young minds translated socks on the floor into good and desirable behavior. They worked hard after that to leave socks in all sorts of exciting places to get that same gleeful reaction from me. (Guess if that worked.)

The Housekeeping Gene is more recessive in them than it is even in me. I figure if newspapers are stacked, dishes and laundry are out of sight, and blankets are pulled up on the bed, the house is clean. They believed if there is walking space, you're okay.

Once one of those folks with the dominant Housekeeping Gene came to visit. She checked under couch cushions and found socks. She wiped her fingers across an end table. She clucked her tongue. "Your life," she said, "would be much happier if only you kept your end tables dusted."

Well, you know how Mary sat at Jesus' feet when He came to visit.[1] Martha got stressed out taking care of things. Jesus let Martha know that it was okay to relax. Housekeeping has no eternal significance. It's not that important. Being with Jesus, soaking up His word, now that's important.

So, if you come to my house and spot dust and cobwebs, don't expect me to scamper for the Pledge® or the lamb's wool duster with the extension wand. If Jesus didn't mind, you shouldn't either.

---

[1] Luke 10 tells the story.

Theology of Dust

On the sixth day God formed man from dust,[2]
Then He said, "This is good."[3]

I figure there's dust enough under my bed
To create a whole neighborhood.[4]

Once, when the Pharisees came to Christ,
He stooped and wrote in the dust[5]

And He could write on our furniture too,
If He just came to visit us.

Dust is prevalent in the Word.
At home, it is unconquerable.

So, please don't mind any dust left behind,
Because dust is theological!

---

[2] Genesis 1:26
[3] Genesis 1:31
[4] Erma Bombeck expressed this thought back in the seventies. I was a teen-ager and pointed it out to Mother. She said God wasn't creating people that way anymore thus dust mopping was not a murderous act.
[5] John 8:6

4

Ashes to Ashes, Dust to Dust

Ecclesiastes 12:7 says that our dust will return to the earth as it was and our spirit will return to God who gave it…

God remembers we are dust[6]
That's the way He created us

But when we step through
Heaven's portal
And with God take on
A life immortal,

We won't be dust
As we sing His praises
Through the heavens,
Through the ages.

His plan for us will be complete
As we nestle there at His feet.

But, I'll be joyful just being
One of God's own

Even if I am only a dust bunny
Under His throne!

---

[6] Psalms 103:14

Domestic

Engineering[7]

---

[7] *Engineering* as in, "This house looks like a train wreck!"

Bless this Mess

It's easy to get discouraged and only see the outward appearance of things.[8] I try to trust God in all things,[9] but tough ones can overwhelm me.[10] I believe God is in control but that 'Let-go-and-let-God' mentality does not come easily to me.

Sometimes I say, "Lord, bless this mess,"
And I mean the world at large.
So much needs God's attention.
Thank God, He's still in charge.

Sometimes I say, "Lord, bless this mess,"
And I'm talking about my home
Or praying about my cooking
Or a relationship gone wrong.

Sometimes I say, "Lord, bless this mess,"
And I'm consulting Him about me.
It seems I have so far to go
And there's just eternity.

But I like this arrangement.
I give God each and every mess
And the more I lay them at His feet,
The more my life is blessed.

---

[8] 1ˢᵗ Samuel 16:7
[9] 1ˢᵗ Timothy 6:17 says that God gives us all good things to enjoy.
[10] Job 13:15 "…though He [God] slay me, yet will I trust Him…" This idea worked real well for Job, but I have a long way to go before I get to that point!

Toilet Bowl Moods

At our house, when you are in a bad temper, full of nastiness and nobody wants to be around you, that's a toilet bowl mood. One day I was in such a mood - cranky and out of sorts.

I ended up in the Old Testament (King James version) on purpose. I was reading the old prophet, Zephaniah. Most of that book is very conducive to toilet bowl moods. There's a lot of gloom and doom and "woe unto you." I was grousing along feeling wicked and obnoxious, thinking, "All right! Go get 'em, God."

Punishment, distress and desolation were perfect for my frame of mind. Then in the third chapter, Zephaniah gets all soft and mushy. The King James Version puts it like this:

The Lord thy God in the midst of thee is mighty,
He will save,
He will rejoice over thee with joy,
He will rest in His love,
He will joy over thee with singing. [11]

It's luscious. God sings. He maybe even hums while He cradles us in His arms. It knocked my spiritual socks off.

---

[11] Zephaniah 3:16b-17

...continued...

When my girls were babies, I sang over them. (Not that day while I was cranky, but on other days.) I made up little songs, like this:

> ♪ *Well, I got two girls - I didn't get no boys,*
> *But my two girls are two little joys*
> *And they are sweet as they can be,*
> *I reckon they take after me!* ♪

The Bible tells us to sing and make melody in our hearts to the Lord.[12]   Jesus sang with the disciples at the last supper.[13] I just never realized that God sang, too. Most parents lullaby their little ones. Discovering that God sang was like getting a kiss on the cheek from heaven.

Nobody ever told me God sang. I never heard a sermon about it. This was news. Exciting news. Someday when I get to heaven, I want to hear His song to me!

I was so pleased that I must have called twenty people that day to ask if they knew God sang. Some did.

One person told me that the verse was only referring to the Israelites in the last days and that it didn't mean that God was going around singing over the rest of us. But if He sang over those rebellious Israelites, surely He would also sing over me. (I can "do" rebellious, too!)

Joy bubbled. I was no longer in a toilet bowl mood. I wondered if God had a heavenly toilet bowl brush for bad moods. How about other spiritual cleaning supplies?   And if He had a spiritual vacuum cleaner for our hearts, would it be a divine Dirt Devil®?

---

[12] Ephesians 5:19
[13] Mark 14:26

God's Vacuum Cleaner

I let sin traipse through my heart.
It left an ugly mess
And so I rearranged myself
To cover things up I guess.

Guilt came in on sin's same path
And dirtied up my soul.
Oh what a trouble I am in,
The song in my heart they stole.

I called on God to help me.
None had ever been un-cleaner. [14]
♪Amazing grace, how sweet the sound! ♪ [15]
God brought His vacuum cleaner!

Guilt and sin are gone in an old dirt bag.
My heart is glad again.
God rejoices in song over me
And I rejoice in Him!

---

[14] Check out Psalms 51:10. The Psalmist must have felt this way too.
[15] John Newton, 1725-1807, wrote the hymn from which these words are taken.

10

The Housekeeping Plan

When Steve and I were first married, I really wanted to be the perfect Susie Homemaker. This was especially difficult since I lacked that dominate Housekeeping Gene.

I was taught as a child to "abstain from all appearance of evil."[16] I assumed that since cleanliness is supposedly next to godliness,[17] then good housekeeping was paramount to Christianity. In order to play it safe, I decided to I ought to shun from the very appearance of messiness, too.

This evolved into the idea that if our front storm door glass was sparkling that people would assume the rest of the house was too. Before too many years passed, my girls innocently and effectively shattered that illusion.

Among the many things that I learned from them, this lesson was one of the most important. You see, the affection in the home is much more important than the appearance of the home.

Great-Aunt Dorey evidently learned this lesson years ago. She told me once that she tried to keep her house clean enough to be healthy and cluttered enough to be happy! Now, that's what I call a profound housekeeping plan.

---

[16] 1st Thessalonians 5:22

[17] By the way, I can't find the idea that cleanliness is next to godliness in the Bible. Did someone just make that up so we would be sinners instead of slobs? Was it merely a ploy for a compulsively clean person to seem more spiritual?

⬯ Kiss the Glass ⬯

I found mouth prints on the storm door glass
All lined up in a row,
So I got out paper towels and cleaner
And tackled that window.
The next morning, walking by,
Guess what I saw that made me sigh?
A whole new row of smears and smudges:
Just a few feet high.

So I marched out my two children
To find the guilty one.
I pointed at the lip prints,
"See what someone has done?"

They were so proud and happy.
Their expressions made that plain.
"No," I told them sternly,
"I just washed that window pane."

But then in all sincerity,
The little one patted my hand.
"Yeah, we know," her sister said,
"That's why we did them again."
"Oh why," I cried, with hands on hips,
"Do you think the door needs prints of lips?"

"But they're for you, Mom, not the door,
So if you need just one kiss more."
Then off they giggled to their play.
I shook my head and put my stuff away,
Thinking,
"Love is shown in the strangest ways,"
And I kissed the glass myself that day.

Born in a Barn

Certain things hang on over generations of time to become traditions. There are things we do and words we say that shape the lives we touch.

One day, we were driving on an old two-lane highway. We have a lot of those in rural Kansas. We passed a grand old barn that had been restored.

I remembered Mother's words when she got after us for leaving the screen door open in the summer. (Of course, that was back when storm doors with mechanical door closers were a luxury we didn't have.) She always said the same thing, "HEY! You weren't born in a barn!"

Now, I only got to say those words of Mother's in winter when kids left the regular door open (due to that automatic apparatus that we have that closes the storm door for us). Now they are adults and I never get to say those words.

So while I was looking at that barn, I thought, "Wow. If you were going to be born in a barn, that would be the barn to be born in."

Then I remembered the One who was born in a barn of sorts. And this is the thought that came to me:

Open Doors

Through the ages carefree children
Have left countless doors ajar

And generations of Mothers have hollered,
"Hey, you weren't born in a barn!"

Now, since Jesus was a child once
And maybe did things children do,

Do you think He was ever human enough
To leave doors open too?

Well, Mothers are seldom speechless
When they're getting after a kid,

But Mary couldn't say that barn thing,
So I wonder what she did?

It probably doesn't matter
But what counts for eternity,

Is Jesus says that He's the door[18]
And He's left himself open for me!

---

[18] John 10:9

Responsibilties

responsibilties

Humpty Dumpty

Jesus tells the story of a master who goes away into a far country.[19] Before he leaves, he calls three servants in. He trusts each one with a gift according to their individual abilities. To one, he gives five talents, to another two, and to the last, one. [20]

The man returns. He calls the servants to bring him his investments. The ones he trusted with the most have used what He gave them wisely. They have increased his outlay. He rewards them for their faithfulness.

Then there is that other fellow. He brings only the one thing that the master gave him. He was careful. He put it away and didn't touch it. He didn't take any chances on losing it. I wonder if this was where the old adage, "Use it or lose it," began. The master takes even that one away and gives it to the servant with the most.

Don't set aside the talent that God has given you.[21]

Humpty Dumpty was lucky.
He had a whole wall.

Some folks only get tight ropes
And crowds watch them fall.

Humpty Dumpty was foolish.
He sat tall out of balance.

He got egg on his face
And he wasted his talents!

---

[19] Matthew 25:14-30

[20] That's what the King James Version calls them. Other versions refer to bags of money or gold.

[21] Henry Van Dyke said, "Use what talents you possess: the woods would be very silent if no birds sang there except those that sang best." ℣

Serve Wholeheartedly [22]

The church we attended decided not to hire a janitor. The money saved was sent to missions. Church folks voluntarily pitched in to do custodial duty on a rotating basis.

We were on the cleaning crew for years. Every year, I would try to talk my husband out of it and he would remind me that our children needed to see us do more than just drop a check in the plate on Sundays. We needed to give that bit of self, too. It was hard to argue with that.

However, I hate cleaning toilets at home, not to mention elsewhere. I would remind myself of David's words when he told Solomon to serve God with a perfect heart and a willing mind.[23] Then I would rationalize that a perfect heart and willing mind would be easier on a royal throne than on a porcelain one…why didn't God call me to be royalty?

I would scold myself because Paul was in prison, cold and chained, and he still told the Philippians to do all things without complaining,[24] while I grouched about a little housekeeping service.

Service is always easier when somebody else does it. I have serious misgivings when it's me. The old hymn, "I Surrender All"[25] brought mental images of me in ultimate surrender waving a toilet bowl brush instead of a white flag.

With many duties, I just have to do the job and trust God to help my attitude. If I wait till things sound like a good idea, life's toilets might never get cleaned.

---

[22] Ephesians 6:7NIV
[23] 1st Chronicles 28:9
[24] Philippians 2:14
[25] J.W. Van DeVenter, 1855-1939

The Tidee Bowl© Man

Perhaps

There is no important thing

And life simply has no meaning

And

We were created on this earth

Because the toilets needed cleaning.

But it says

Right in the Word that for us

God has a plan,[26]

So for now

I strive to be content[27]

As the Tidee Bowl™ man!

---

[26] Jeremiah 29:11-12

[27] My goal is to be able to say (like Paul in Philippians 4:11) that I have learned to be content in any circumstance.

Dirty Work[28]

Jesus compared the kingdom of heaven to a shepherd and his flock.[29] He talks about the constant care required and  how a good shepherd would give his life for his sheep. It is a relationship based on trust. The sheep trust the shepherd to take care of them. They know his voice. He trusts the sheep to follow him.

I don't know much about animals, but I know Don. He's a farmer. He raises cows.   His cows trust him and he can't quit meeting their needs just because it's a certain day. Jesus tackles such a dilemma with the Pharisees when the disciples ate on the Sabbath.[30] Common sense and loving God mattered more than rules and rituals.

One rainy Sunday, Don's wife sat alone at church. During the sermon, he quietly slipped into the pew beside her. Later, we found out where he had been...

Pulling a calf on Sunday morning
In the rain, boots deep in mud

Grimed and slimed from head to toe
In mucus, sweat and blood.

Then headed for the showers.
Barely time to get to church.

God gets to rest on Sundays[31]
A farmer still does dirty work!

---

[28] Skip this page if you have a weak stomach.
[29] John 10
[30] Matthew 12:1-8
[31] Genesis 2:2

19

Forget Cheese!

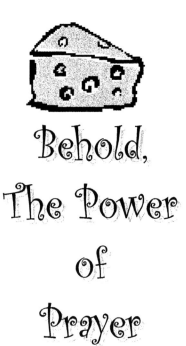

Behold,
The Power
of
Prayer

Jesus Calls Us[32]

Our children were educated in public schools. During their grade school years, we were involved in the parent-teacher organization.

There, I met a fellow believer. Usually every believer is another lesson in who God is.

At the time, I was very unorganized. I constantly lost my keys. It was often like an Easter egg hunt when it was time to leave home. One day, the hunt was unsuccessful. I just had to say, "Help, God! I did it again."

I meant to do the prayer thing right, but the phone was ringing. I was in a "Let's make a deal" mood. I thought if I didn't answer the phone, and I kept looking and praying, that God would recognize my great sacrifice and take care of me.

Besides, I really didn't want to talk then anyway. (Some sacrifice, huh?) I needed to go meet that woman for our project work. I just kept on looking and the phone just kept on ringing.

Of course, this was **B.C.I. (Before Caller ID)** for us, so I couldn't peek and then decide not to answer. Finally, when I couldn't stand the incessant noise anymore, I decided it must be an important call.

I told God the deal was off and went to answer the phone. Just as I got to it, it quit ringing, but guess what was right there beside it?

---

[32] Cecil F. Alexander, 1818-1895, penned a hymn that starts out, " Jesus calls us." Quite honestly, the lyrics have nothing to do with telephones, but I wanted to borrow the title.

...continued...

*It was time
To do
The happy dance!*

I thought this was the answer to my prayer, a fulfillment of that scripture that says, "Before they call, I will answer."[33] (Only, maybe God called in answer to my call!") I was so pleased…a kiss on the cheek from God.

 When I got to my meeting, I told that gal. She was shocked to find out that I was one of those petty people who take up all God's time, dragging Him through the jumble of my life and expecting Him to fix every little thing.

Until then, I thought that anybody who numbered the hairs on my head,[34] saw each sparrow fall[35] and kept my tears in a bottle[36] wouldn't have any trouble helping out with everyday aggravations. (You know, the baloney of life…)

I forgot about the verses that said to cast all your care upon Him,[37] and that the Lord is the place to go when trouble comes.[38] I only saw the logic of her words. I was guilty.

I had inconvenienced God.

---

[33] Isaiah 65:24
[34] Matthew 10:30
[35] Matthew 10:29
[36] Psalms 56:8
[37] 1st Peter 5:7
[38] Nahum 1:7

Prayer Lines

"Don't clog up the prayer lines,"
My friend said that to me.

She said God had more important things
To do than meet my needs.

She said to save my praying
For big stuff...like world peace...

That God wouldn't ever get anything done
If He's out looking for my keys.

I went home feeling guilty.
I hung my head in shame.

I asked God to forgive me
For all the times I called His name.

I quit praying about my troubles:
Tried to make it on my own.

Out loud, I prayed for the big stuff,
Inside, I only groaned.[39]

---

[39] Romans 8:27

...continued...

God understood my groaning:
He knew the words I would not say,

And God who numbers the hair on my head[40]
Heard the prayer I never prayed.

"You can't clog up the prayer lines,"
I thought I heard Him say gently,

"And sometimes even little things
Mean something big to me."

Well, my friend has long since moved away,
But I pray someday she'll see,

You can't clog up the prayer lines...

God's
Bigger than the
phone
company!

---

[40] Matthew 10:30

Old Movies

Late night black-and-white movies have been in vogue at our house since before we had children. It all started because I thought Roy Rogers was a myth like Paul Bunyan.

My hubby, Steve insisted that Roy was a real person. I supposed Roy was an Old Western figment of modern imagination. We stayed up till wee hours of the night to settle it. Imagine my surprise to find out how real Roy really was. I learned my reality was not necessarily authentic truth. (But maybe Roy was a kind of myth…or at least a legend in his own time!)

I had never seen <u>Singin' in the Rain</u>, <u>Pollyanna</u>, <u>Oklahoma</u>, or <u>It's a Wonderful Life</u>. Thus began a great tradition of broadening my television horizons.

This brings us to <u>The FBI Story,</u> an old black and white movie that starred Jimmy Stewart. It was a propaganda film for what was then a new government agency. His character's son dies in the midst of a prayer. To comfort his grieving wife, Stewart says it was the best possible way to die: the son got to finish his talk with God in person. What a great thought!

One morning, one of my girls and I were driving together. A man on the radio was talking about his special procedure for prayer…using this method would guarantee results. I turned it off. I listen to Christian radio a lot, so my daughter asked why.

I told her Jesus didn't limit us to certain formulas. He told us that all things we asked in prayer, believing, we would receive.[41] Rules about prayer should only be guidelines. You can't make God do your will by praying a certain way. If it worked that way, God would be a genie, not God.

---

[41] Matthew 21:22

Face-to-Face

Jesus used what we call The Lord's Prayer[42]
To teach us how to pray

But the thief on the cross didn't use it
And he got answered anyway.[43]

Jesus healed the sick, the lame and blind
Because they each had faith

And that was more important
Than what they did or didn't say.

You don't have to rub God's belly
Or carefully tickle His ears

Because He will answer even prayers
That don't use words[44]*---just tears---*

Praying is contact with God.[45]
No matter the time or place.

And if you start a prayer and die,
You get to finish it face to face.

---

[42] Matthew 6:9-13
[43] Matthew 23:42-43
[44] Psalms 34:17
[45] Ignatius of Loyola said that everything that one turns in the direction of God is prayer.

We're

On The

U

P

W

A

R

D

Trail

The Loop Verse

Isaiah 30:18 TLB says *"...the Lord still waits for you to come to Him so He can show you His love, He will comfort you to bless you just as He has said. Blessed are those who wait on the Lord."*

It starts out with the Lord waiting for you to come to Him and then ends with you waiting for Him.

It used to drive me crazy, like I was waiting here while God was waiting there and nothing was happening anywhere. I would pray about something without result. I would wonder if I was in the wrong place while He was elsewhere, waiting for me.

Then I wrote this poem about an entirely different subject and realized it did approximately the same thing. It looped. We waited downstairs while our kids waited upstairs until the time was right for all of us to get together.

I got that "ah ha" feeling. God waits for us to pray and we wait for Him to answer. He doesn't barge without an invitation. He's pretty polite about intruding in our lives.

 Praying is like calling a taxi. Taxis don't always just show up when you need them (although they often do). Taxis wait for our call...or whistle or wave. God longs for us to do the same for Him.

Freewill requires us to choose Him as our transport. Sometimes, He is right there, and all we have to do is look up. Other times, we wait. Sometimes, we choose to walk away without Him.

God taught me that occasionally we do have to wait upon the Lord[46] while He is waiting on us. Then when everything is in its proper place, and at the proper time, all things do work together for good.[47]

Just like when it is bedtime for the children...

---

[46] Isaiah 40:31
[47] Romans 8:28

Is there anybody up here that I love?

When age dictated it was time
To adopt more modest ways,
Their dad and I would wait downstairs
While our girls put on p-jays.

They'd wait for us to come to them
When it was time for bed:
To tell them stories, tuck them in
And kiss them on the head.

They'd always hear our footprints
But to announce that we were come,
I'd pause and ask, "Is there anybody
Up here that I love?"

Almost always they said, "Yes,"
For me that was enough.
Permission granted. Entrance allowed.
Oh, what we do for love!

And when God dictates it's time for me
To leave this life I know
And dressed in Christ's own righteousness,
I stand before God's throne,[48]

I know He will understand my habit,
To pause when I am come,
To ask again, "Is there anybody
Up here that I love?"

I pray to hear a resounding "YES!"
That'll be enough for me.
Permission granted. Entrance allowed.
To love eternally.

---

[48] Revelations 7:13-14

At the Top

As members of God's family, we will someday have a home in heaven where we will rest in God's love. Right now, as members of an earthly family, we live in an old house on a brick street. It used to have vines covering it. In winter, they lost their leaves. Then it looked like our house had varicose veins. The vines grew through the walls into the upstairs. At a glance, they looked like lovely hanging potted plants...without the pots of course. They were the only growing things I ever had much success with. We tore them out, but in retrospect, perhaps we should have kept them.

Our bedrooms are upstairs as was common a hundred plus years ago. There is a certain freedom that comes from keeping the sleeping area separate from the living area. (And it isn't just the housekeeping thing, either!) It's the same release that comes from leaving your work at work. You've done all you can do for the day. It's a separation of one part of life from another.

Our bedroom is at the top of the stairs,
I like it there just so
Each night when I head up to bed,
I leave my troubles down below.

I leave them there
In God's own care,
Just beside
The bottom stair,

Then pray the Lord
My soul to keep
And peacefully
Drift off to sleep.

30

Alternative Bedtime Prayer

Sometimes I do not leave my troubles down below (or perhaps they slip up the stairs behind me). Then, my prayers become pout-prayers. I want God to fix everything. He often lets me live with consequences of my blunders. This causes me to quibble with Him about our respective roles. He has an extreme advantage at such times: He is God.

The Psalmist was also whined on occasion. In Psalms 6, David tells God not to be mad at him. He says how weak and troubled he is. He pretty much lets God know to get back there and save him. He says that he is worn out from groaning, that he makes his bed swim with tears.[49]

Wow. Through all that, God still loved him. He doesn't berate him for praying wrong. When we pour our hearts out to God, He listens and loves us.

God gets me through the doleful days and the joyful ones. The Bible says the Lord gives strength to his people[50] and that weeping may endure for a night, but joy comes in the morning.[51] (No wonder doctors used to say, "Take two aspirin and call me in the morning." They knew that God starts most of our mornings with joy.)

So, be sure you don't stop praying just because you are down. God will listen…and if He doesn't change your trouble, perhaps He will change you!

Now I lay down wide-awake.
I pray the Lord my troubles take.
But, if He won't, I pray for class to
Endure whatever I am asked to!

---

[49]The most I've ever done is get my pillow wet. I must be very blessed.
[50] Psalms 29:11
[51] Psalms 30:5

*"The Lord
is
my Rock..."*

Psalms 18: 2

Rock Talk

When you are the mother of teen-age daughters, it is an incredible high to have them borrow your clothes. It is like getting the Good Housekeeping Seal of Approval©, only better.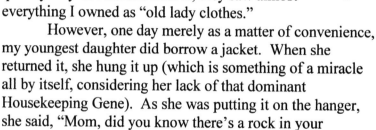

My girls went through this stage very quickly. By late middle school, they saw almost everything I owned as "old lady clothes."

However, one day merely as a matter of convenience, my youngest daughter did borrow a jacket. When she returned it, she hung it up (which is something of a miracle all by itself, considering her lack of that dominant Housekeeping Gene). As she was putting it on the hanger, she said, "Mom, did you know there's a rock in your pocket?"

Well, I did know. Carried one for years. Can't remember when or exactly how I started doing it. Just that the first of many rocks was triangular and I carried it long enough to wear it smooth and darken its color. Then I lost it during a difficult situation.

I can remember fussing at God that life was hard and that losing with my special rock was a real problem. And what was I supposed to hold onto? (I don't always make sense...I forgot I was supposed to hold onto to Him!)

I eventually learned that it wasn't hanging on to a rock that was important. However, it was a tangible reminder of...

Oh, I'm getting ahead of myself. In response to her question, I said, "Yes." I knew I had a rock in my pocket. And she asked why.

The answer didn't rhyme when I told her that day, but of course it does now.

Rock in my Pocket

*I carry a rock in my pocket
To remind me that God carries me[52]*

*Through all the good and the bad times.
He has since Calvary.*

*I carry a rock in my pocket
To remind me that God is my rock,[53]*

*My refuge[54] and my salvation:[55]
He's all I've really got.*

*Maybe I'm just a rock in God's pocket,
A simple and rough, gray stone,*

*But He keeps smoothing and polishing me:[56]
Making me one of His own.*

*Some folks don't understand that.
They're filled with doubt and dread*

*Because they don't carry God in their hearts
And they carry their rocks in their heads!*

---

[52] Isaiah 41:10
[53] Psalms 92:15
[54] Psalms 91:2
[55] Psalms 25:5
[56] Philippians 1:6

Rock of Ages

The Bible is full of rocks. In Numbers 20, when the people are grouching about lack of water, God tells Moses to get the Israelites together and speak to a certain rock. Moses loses his temper, calls the people rebels and hits the rock, but God still uses that rock to provide water for the people.

In the New Testament, Paul tells about Moses and that Rock. He says that Rock was Christ.[57] The Psalmist often said God was His rock.[58] Jesus tells us the wise man built his house upon the rock.[59]

Jesus asked the disciples who they thought He was. Peter answered that He was Christ, Son of God. He spoke in faith. Christ replied that He would build His church upon that rock.[60] Some people think He meant Peter's solid faith. Others think He meant Peter himself. Either way, it was a significant compliment that Peter returns later when He says Jesus is the living stone.[61]

Then this legacy is passed on to us. He says we are lively[62] stones, being built into a spiritual house...acceptable to God because of Jesus Christ.

That makes me want to be a building block that He can use in His construction plan. Don't you want to be a lively rock, too?

---

[57] 1st Corinthians 10:4

[58] Psalms 28:1, Psalms 31:3, Psalms 42:9, Psalms 62:2 & 7, Psalms 71:3, Psalms 89:26, Psalms 92:15, Psalms 94:22, Psalms 95:1 and there are probably more, but you get the idea

[59] Luke 6:48

[60] Matthew 16:15-18

[61] 1st Peter 2:4

[62] 1st Peter 2:5 the King James Version says *lively*. Other versions say living. I like *lively*, it is more animated and joyful, isn't it? It's a big step past merely existing.

God Almighty

God Almighty,
Voice of Thunder,[63]
You are the Rock[64]
I now hide under.

God, whose voice can calm the wind,[65]
Please speak in tones I'll comprehend.

God our Father, strong to save,
Whose hand has stilled the restless wave,[66]

Whose touch has healed,[67] whose love has raised,[68]
Where do sinners find Your grace?[69]

I've searched books galore on countless shelves.
I've searched the church and inside myself.

Somewhere in life, I missed Your gift,
Swept by life's waves, I am a-drift.

God, I've been diligent and ardent:
I just want to touch the hem of Your garment.[70]

Gentle Shepherd, can You see my heart?
Hold it now. How great Thou art![71]

---

[63] Psalms 29:3
[64] Psalms 92:15
[65] Matthew 8:26
[66] Psalms 89:9
[67] Luke 13:11-13
[68] John 11:38-44
[69] Psalms 34:4
[70] Like the woman in Luke 8:43-48
[71] 1st John 4:4KJV, "…greater is He that is in you than He that is in the world."

A Pebble in your Shoe

I am married to my best friend. We have been living and working together for most of our wedded life. He figured out a long time ago that I wasn't perfect and stuck around anyway. We figure we have clocked more hours together than most couples that have been married twice as long as we have. I consider it one of God's greatest gifts that this man still loves me!

He notices when a thought is good. It is a marvelous thing when he says, "Honey, that ought to be a poem." For me, that's better than a box of chocolates!

He might have gotten the short end of the marriage stick though. I am not really the huggy-bear, kissy-poo, hearts-and-roses type, but I am absolutely blessed to be his wife.

I thought that I could be your rock.
That's what I set out to do.
Instead it seems that I became
A pebble in your shoe.

As a rock, I am inadequate,
I never could deny it:
But David didn't use a boulder
When he killed Goliath.

So though I'm not a mighty rock,
I'd like to stay with you,
Just in case a giant comes
And a little rock'll do!

When life hands you lemons

Pucker up!

Sleeping Late

Some poems are inspired by deep theological thought. This one isn't. It's not even mildly spiritual. When we moved into this old house, dozens of pigeons frequented here. They were nuisances. They left nasty droppings. In our remodeling, we sided over the open eaves and their sitting places disappeared.

I do not miss their mess, but I do miss their song. I have never purposely been an early riser. I was never ready for their morning melodies. They were such early birds... sometimes even earlier than the sun. Looking back, I realize it was so much lovelier to be serenaded awake than to be startled into reality by a shrill alarm buzzer. I didn't realize they were blessings.

I wake to pigeons cooing,
Wooing love beneath my eaves.
I wake to breezes rushing
Through ancient oak tree leaves.

I wake to dawn's light breaking
Through tangled threads of sleep.
I close my eyes, my sleep to keep,
The pigeons scream,
The wind's a shriek!

Clouds threaten me!
I dare not peek!
Leave me alone!
I want to sleep
...A hundred years...
...A day...an hour?
Oh what's the use?
My mouth tastes sour.

The 1000 Year Long Day

When I start a day without enough rest, the whole world seems out of balance. If I don't take to check in with God, I lose control. Nothing goes right.

Pierre de Coubertin must have had a day like that when he said, "The important thing in life is not the triumph but the struggle."

"...A day with the Lord is as a thousand years,
And a thousand years is as a day..."[72]

God, my day seemed just that long.
Everything I did went wrong.

Usually I think, "It's all for the good,"[73]
Because "God has a plan."[74]
Today I think that Murphy's law
Must be the twelfth command.

Jesus added, "Love each other,"[75]
To the ten You wrote in stone.
Murphy said that whatever can
Always will go wrong.

I followed Your eleven laws.
They were no problem, You see,

But on this 1000 year long day,
Murphy followed me!

---

[72] II Peter 3:8
[73] Romans 8:28
[74] Jeremiah 29:11-12
[75] John 13:34

Counting Sheep

1st Corinthians 1:9 KJV begins with the words, "God is faithful." When my troubles overwhelm me, I rely on that faithfulness. Even when I am too defeated to sleep or pray, and all I have are those groanings, [76] He often comforts me.

I was troubled one night.
I couldn't sleep.
I fretted long hours.
I counted sheep.

Our Lord must have heard me
Tossing in bed
'Cause I don't remember
A prayer being said,

But comfort came later
– Oh merciful sleep –
I dreamed I saw Jesus
With all of those sheep.

Gracious and gentle,
The kind Shepherd said,
"Don't count on these,
Count your blessings instead."

So, next time I'm tired
And I just can't sleep,
I'll ♫count my many blessings♫ [77]
And leave my worries at Jesus' feet!

---

[76] Romans 8:26
[77] Johnson Oatman, Jr. (1856-1926) wrote the hymn "Count your Blessings." One line says, "Count your many blessings, name them one by one and it will surprise you what the Lord has done…" I wonder if he intended the countdown as a relaxation technique!

God Counts Sheep, too

The Word says that
God never slumbers,[78]
But whenever He's counting His sheep,[79]

Oh Lord, I want to be one
Of those numbers

Yes! I am counting on God counting me![80]

---

[78] Psalms 121:4 says God neither sleeps nor slumbers. I reckon that means He works the day shift and the night shift!

[79] Psalms 95:7 says we are the people of His pasture and the sheep of His hand.

[80] In Luke 23:42, this is approximately what the thief on the cross said when he asked Jesus to remember him when He came into His kingdom.

Cap'n Crunch®

As the girls were growing up, mornings at our house were often a cross between the Indy 500 and a demolition derby...fast and furious! As they got older, I learned it was better for me to just stay out of the way. When everyone else was gone, I was blessed to officially start my day.

I sat alone at breakfast,
A Bible by my bowl.
I thought that I would feed my face
While God fed my soul.

I skimmed through verses restlessly.
My eyes wandered off with my thoughts.
Soon I found me reading
The side of the cereal box.

Now if you think Christianity
Hasn't got much punch,
Then you never compared the nutritional facts
Between God and Cap'n Crunch™

With the Cap'n, you count calories.
With God, you count blessings untold.
The Cap'n satisfies the stomach.
God fortifies the soul.

So I turned back toward the Bible
In a really hungry mood
And thanked God for my daily bread
And for His real "soul food."

Pepto Bismol™

I have never developed proper eating habits. As I age, I get to pay for this lack of discipline more and more.

I like cinnamon buns and soda pop
First thing in the morning when I get up.

When lunch rolls around, I try to think thin
Over carry out pizza that I carry in.

 Then a chocolate malt
or a strawberry shake
For my afternoon coffee break,

And to fend off any possible craving,
There are two chocolate bars
That I hid and I'm saving.

For this self-indulgence,
Some think I should suffer,
But I've learned that's
What they make the pink stuff fer!

The

Gift

Of

Hospitality

Dropping By

I don't always pay enough attention to etiquette. I don't even own Miss Manner's book of rules about proper decorum. Mostly, I just wing it on common sense and kindness.

We went bike riding one evening. (On occasion, Steve does bike with me.) We were across town, near some friends' house. On a whim, we decided to stop by and no, we didn't call first. I left a note under a rock by the front step...

We came by to visit you.
We found that you were gone.

So we sat down on your porch and
Admired your lovely lawn.

The evening wasn't wasted.
We had a lovely time.

We rocked and talked and reminisced.
We watched the pale moon rise.

So thanks for your hospitality
Though you were not in.

Next time let us know before you go.
We just might come again!

Tea Bags

I do love a cup of tea. I like clove tea or a plain blend of black and orange pekoe tea. I do not like milk or lemon in my tea, but I do love it sweet. And, contrary to popular consensus, I don't really mind drop in company to share it with. It is seldom even scary anymore – since the kids are grown, there's not all those socks and dust bunnies lying around.

Tea bags are waiting in the kitchen
In hopes you'll visit me.

This old house is cleaned and dusted.
Now it wants some company.

I've got cookies baked for munching
And fresh fruit in a basket...

But I don't see you coming...

I guess I should have asked ya.

Satin Sheets

Shortly after we were married, Steve's grandparents came several hundred miles to visit us. They must have read Emily Post. They called ahead.

I wanted to treat them like royalty. I wanted them to love me. I wanted to give them the best we had. We had gotten some lovely sheets as a wedding gift. We decided they would be the first ones to use them. I laundered those sheets and made the bed. The rest, as they say, is history.

We put Grandma and Grandpa in our bed
When they came for a stay.
We decked it in the satin sheets
Given us on our wedding day.

We really hadn't used them yet
Or we'd have never put them on.
The trouble started when the folks got in
And didn't end till dawn.

Grandpa rolled to say good night.
Grandma slipped right through his arms.
The blankets slid off whenever they moved.
Those sheets weren't worth a darn.

Grandpa slept as stiff as a board.
He couldn't even move his head
'Cause if he did, he said his pillow
Just shot right off the bed!

But in the night they slid too close
And Grandma couldn't breathe
So she held onto the bedpost
And gave a mighty heave.

Well, those slick sheets did their stuff.
Grandpa woke up on the floor
And though they laughed whenever they told it,
They didn't stay here anymore!

Faith

In

Focus

Faith

Mother Teresa said, *"God never gives us more than we can bear, but sometimes I wish He didn't trust me quite so much."* However, she was worthy of trust. She preached the gospel with her actions instead of just with her words.[81]

It is hard for me, an ordinary believer, safe in my regular life with my normal job and conventional home, to even imagine the hardships and living conditions that she dealt with everyday. She had faith. God worked things out. He does that. He keeps us involved in the solutions to our problems. He forgives sins, but doesn't necessarily rescue us from their consequences.

 He seldom sends money to solve financial difficulties, although He may help us find ways to earn it. He gives us the strength to bear our troubles, but He doesn't necessarily do the Calgon© thing and take us away...even though it would sure be nice now and then...

Joseph Girzone, the man who blessed my life with the modern day parable, Joshua,[82] wrote, "Just try to do your best. God always understands if you try." Faith is all about the effort of believing. Faith is putting elbow grease into your prayers and doing what you can with what God gives you to work with.

Mother Teresa was the kind of person she was because her faith had works. Even though we know that it is by grace that we are saved through faith,[83] we also know that faith without works is dead.[84]

---

[81] Saint Francis of Assisi said, "Preach the Gospel at all times. If necessary, use words."
[82] Joshua, Joseph Girzone, Doubleday, New York, NY, 1994
[83] Ephesians 2:8
[84] James 2:17

A Mountain in my Life

I
Had a
Mountain in my life
And faith as a mustard seed,

So by faith
I commanded that mountain
To be cast into the sea.

I claimed
The Biblical promises.
I waited for God on bended knee.

Then at last
I got an answer from Him:
He dropped a shovel to me.

One scoop
At a time that mountain
Is disappearing as I had prayed.

Faith in God
May move a mighty mountain
But sometimes faith must use a spade!

Leap of Faith

Sometimes I am convinced I know exactly what God wants me to do. Then, everything goes wrong. Those times, I wish it could be as easy as finding God in a burning bush.

"When God closes a door, look for a window."
I hope those words are right,

Because doors keep closing in my face
And there's no hinges or knobs in sight.

I'm not pious but I have been spending time
In prayer --- down on all fours ---

I'm covering all the bases I can:
Checking for hatches and doggie doors.

They say, "The Lord helps those who help themselves,"[85]
And "Faith without works is dead."[86]

So by faith (just in case I'm on the top floor),
I'm knotting sheets from off the bed.

My frail human side fears the unknown (and heights),
God knows that is the truth,
So if I must make a leap of faith,

I want a Parachute!

---

[85] Actually, I don't know who "they" are, but honest, here where I live, people do say this.
[86] James 2:20 this idea shows up a lot, doesn't it?

Walk by Faith

In Mark 9 a man brings his son to Jesus to have an evil spirit cast out. Jesus tells the man that all things are possible if he can believe. The man responds by saying, "Lord, I believe: help thou mine unbelief."[87]

Once, Jesus and the disciples were in a boat. Jesus fell asleep in the lower part of the boat. A terrible storm blew up. They grew fearful and came and woke him.

He went out and calmed the storm, but he questioned them, "Why are you fearful, O ye of little faith?"[88] The second half of that sentence seems to answer the question in the first half, don't you think?

"We walk by faith and not by sight."[89]
But sometimes I forget

And I focus on the troubles
Not on the things God meant.

I've tried walking with my eyes shut
But shame on me, I peek

Because even though I want to trust[90]
I have a doubting streak.

---

[87] Mark 9:24KJV
[88] Matthew 8:26KJV
[89] II Corinthians 5:7
[90] Mark 9:23-24

Let's

Get

Physical!

My Bicycle

Steve was seven when he got his first paper route. He rode a bike and threw papers for years. For him, a bicycle was drudgery.

For me, a bicycle meant freedom. It was a natural extension of sunshine, blue skies and balmy breezes. I was enamored with the wind. I didn't understand the dynamics of biking, but I had balance and I loved to ride.

God used to sit on my handlebars
Whenever I'd ride my bike.
He would puff His breath at me
That was the part that I liked.

The faster I'd go,
The harder He'd blow
And my hair would fly in His wind
And even though I never saw Him,
I loved to ride with my friend.

Then at school I learned about
Aerodynamics and wind resistance
And God quit riding my handlebars
At my educated insistence.

I'd go visit Him on Sundays.
Sit in church on the organ side,
But I never felt that swelling joy
That I felt with Him when we'd ride.

Well, now I'm older and wiser
And my driveway is home to two cars,
But I still find myself out riding my bike
And God's back on my handlebars.

Dumbbell

When I was in gym class, we did feminine stuff like running laps around the basketball court and little tumbling routines. We did these things slowly so we wouldn't work up a sweat.

Times have changed. Exercise programs have changed. Our girls had weight lifting in Physical Education classes in high school. They even used real weights.

There's an old saying, "Horses sweat and men perspire, but ladies only glow." Well, we never wanted to get past that glowing stage. And we never lifted a barbell.

In my walk as a believer I tend to lug around a lot of excess weight. Probably the only thing I have that God has not given me is the baloney that I chose to drag around. And what in the world do I want it for?

Jesus says if we are weighed down with excess burdens, He will give us rest.[91] He says His *yoke* is easy.[92] (And He's not talking about how He likes His eggs, kids!) And He says His burden is light.[93] It just takes a little faith to let Him have our heavy weights!

---

[91] Matthew 11:28

[92] A yoke in Jesus time was a big wooden framework that hooked over a couple of oxen so they'd have to work together. Yoke refers figuratively to His willingness to work with us. His tender mercy and grace partner with us to make us strong.

[93] Matthew 11:30

Weight Lifters

Weight lifters show mighty strength by holding
Heavy barbells way up high.
They pump it up
To show they're tough.
They make it look easy as pie.

I try to do that with my troubles.
I lift them up high in prayer.
But sometimes I can't loosen my grip and
I get stuck just holding them there.

Part of me wants God to work His plan.
Part of me fears to let go.
God might not do what I want Him to
Or my burden might land on a toe.

So if I struggle to hold bar bell burdens
When God would call them His,
Perhaps the relevant question is
Which one the dumbbell is?

The Word says, "Cast all your care on Him,"[94]
And that's what I want to do
Because He's the Greatest Weight Lifter of all and
He'll lift my burdens, too!

---

[94] 1st Peter 5:7

Shape Up

I want to go jogging. I want to get thin.
But I can't because of the shape that I'm in.
The shape that I'm in does not glide along lithely.
Instead it just bounces along rather ripply.

I thought about swimming. Whales do it a lot.
But they don't wear suits and I'd rather not
Be seen in a suit or be seen in just skin
Oh, darn this fat that I've sandwiched me in.

Yes, I thought of aerobics and all I can say
Is I'd feel like a cow trying to do the ballet.

Well, I need to start something.
Guess I'll just take a stroll...

Right after I finish this cinnamon roll!

My newest and most favorite all time excuse for not worrying about my exercise and eating habits is found in Proverbs 28:25KJV where it says, "*...but he that putteth his trust in the Lord shall be made fat.*" Now other versions of the Bible say stuff about trusting and prospering, but this is one of those times that I want to stick to the 15th century English!

Multi-Purpose Head Gear

Most of the time, I try to be on target Biblically. I don't want to confuse or misuse God's word. So, before you are exposed to the following poem, I do want to warn you that it is not anything that could be justified through Scripture.

You know how folks used to say we needed to polish up our neighbor's halo...well, I may be the neighbor whose halo is going to need a little extra shine!

As a child I tried to figure out how God was going to keep heaven happy. I had trouble sitting still through church: I knew that if I had to sit still through eternity, I was going to be in trouble. Then I figured it out (I thought)...God's eternal entertainment...

I don't want to set my sights too high
And then be disappointed,
But truth is I'm hoping when I die,
My headgear won't be pointed.

I don't want horns or a tail.
I look terrible in red.
If I haven't earned a crown below,
I'm hoping that instead

On judgment day, with sins forgiven,
I'll hear the saints a-singing
And standing by the gates of heaven,
I'll see the angels winging.

Oh, I have been practicing wearing a hat,
Hoping someday God would give me

A simple, versatile halo that
Could double for a Frisbee.©

Walk in the Rain

The Bible tells us to walk in the spirit,[95] but some - times, I walk in the rain. I do not like rain from inside the house. I don't think Solomon liked it very much either. He compared constant dripping on a rainy day to an irritable woman.[96]

That little soft pit-pat noise that rain makes on the roof turns me into one of those women Solomon talked about, so I am better off to go walk in the rain.

I have never prayed that God would only let it rain at certain times, but I've sure wanted to. That verse about asking amiss[97] is my assurance that I'd be wasting God's time and my own. But in daylight hours, I enjoy umbrellas, puddles and the memories that wet weather elicits.

I took a walk when it rained one day
And all the worms came out to play.
Seeing them I reminisced
On when my brother picked
Them up with sticks.

I'd run from him terrified.
Now we're both grown
And dignified.

We don't 'do' worms.
We don't wade while it's pouring.
Isn't being a grown-up boring?

---

[95] Galatians 5:16
[96] Proverbs 27:15
[97] James 4:3

Looking

For

God

Check the Bushes

I grew up in a church. I learned God was Almighty. I was aware of His power and might. Sort of. Somehow, the older I got, the more mixed up I got. I thought God was unpredictable and unreliable.

For a long time, I did not realize it was the beliefs that were goofed up, not God. I gave Him my heart as a child, but by my teen years, I trusted him less and less. I got God tangled up in stuff that wasn't Biblical. I believed fearfully and tried to keep the fear hidden. I longed for God's favor and feared for His notice. As an adult, I am still learning to see Him, just as He is.

I used to check under the bushes
Just in case God might be there.
I thought Moses knew best
How to worship - out in the open air -

Moses had no stained glass windows,
No walls, not even a pew,
He got to hear God really talking[98]
And he wasn't in Sunday school!

Some people hunt four leaf clovers.
Some check for change in pay phone slots.
But me? I just check the bushes
'Cause I'm still searching for God.[99]

---

[98] Exodus 3 tells the story of the burning bush.
[99] Isaiah 55:6 says to seek the Lord while He may be found.

Wind in my Face

You can't love the great outdoors and live in the Midwest without learning to appreciate the wind. The Psalmist tells us that God makes His wind to blow.[100] It is evidently an activity He enjoys, because He certainly keeps it moving around here!

Something
In the wind
Makes me want to turn and face it:

Arms out-stretched
As if somehow I could catch it
And embrace it.

Expectantly
I pirouette
Hoping I will see

God there
With His cheeks puffed out
Eyes twinkling at me.

---

[100] Psalms 147:18

Skipping Church

My first concept of God was as my invisible, invincible friend, my perfect playmate and protector...not much different than my Dust Bunny friends. I loved and trusted Him. I thought I made a difference in God's life. Our camaraderie was absolute. This poem encompasses what Paul said about being a child and understanding as a child.[101]

Church was dark and gloomy
When I was just a kid
And I felt bad for God because
The grown-ups locked Him in.
So I snuck in one sunny day
And asked God to come out and play.

All those grown-ups had shut their eyes,
They didn't even realize
That God was gone outside to play with me,
To somersault and climb a tree,
Oh, I squealed with glee
At hide'n'seek
'Cause even though He didn't peek,
God always knew exactly
Where I'd be!
We tiptoed along old railroad tracks.
We hop scotched over sidewalk cracks.
We watched the clouds flat on our backs,
Until the church bells clatter-clacked.

Then it was time to go join in
The dreary prayer and reverent hymn,
Oh, but that was my best service ever,
When God and I skipped church together!

---

[101] 1st Corinthians 13:11

Spice

Of

Life

Salt of the Earth

God might be a salt-aholic. In the Word, it says we believers are the salt of the earth,[102] and there are so many of us, it makes me think that God likes lots of salt.

God says we are the Salt of the Earth
And oh I think that's better
Than if He had to sneeze in church
Because we were the pepper!

God's Marketing Plan

You don't have to be perfect to be part of God's marketing plan. Peter was part of it and he wasn't perfect. He denied Christ three times.[103] He must have felt like a failure after that, because he headed back to be a fisherman.[104]

After the resurrection, Jesus went to find Peter. Peter was too excited to row back to shore. He jumped in the water to swim to Christ. Later, Jesus asked Peter if he loved Him. Three times, Peter says yes, just like the three denials. I like to think that each affirmation of his love helped to heal the corresponding denial.

Each time that Peter said, "Yes," Jesus commanded him to feed His sheep. Before the crucifixion Peter failed because of his mouth, but on the day of Pentecost,[105] he used that same mouth to boldly proclaim the Christ he had denied. Peter fed those sheep that Christ commanded him to feed.

Peter was Salt...so are we!

---

[102] Matthew 5:13
[103] Mark 14:72
[104] Mark 21:3
[105] Acts 2

Movie Show

When you go to the movie show,
You buy popcorn to eat
And truth to tell,
They salt it well
So you'll need to buy a drink.

As believers,
Just like that,
We are sent to create a thirst,
So shake it up wherever you go,
Because you are the Salt of the Earth.

Then when the lost are thirsting,
Parched to their very core,
Christ comes as
The Living Water[106]

And He gives till they thirst no more.

---

[106] John 4:10

Stepping
in
the

Light

Walk like an Egyptian

I thought that Christianity meant I could have it all:
Smile when heartaches happened & walk without a fall.
Well, I can walk like an Egyptian,
a lady or a duck

But spiritually, I often limp in a religious rut.

Troubles come and heartaches happen.
They often make me grieve.
So I whine and remind the Lord
To take better care of me.

I pouted, " Lord, last Sunday at church I sang a hymn
I didn't even fall asleep when Pastor preached on sin!"

"God," I said, "see what I've done and
What did you do for me?
You let all these problems come
And inconvenience me..."

God's gracious. He let me vent until one day I realized
That He went out on a limb for me: because of me He died.

So maybe Christianity doesn't mean I get it all
And religion will not save me when I slip and fall.

But God is there and that's the difference
That a Christian walk can be,
Especially when I walk in the truth
Of Jesus who loves me.

Now when I'm discouraged, I try to remember this,
It isn't <u>how</u> I'm walking; it's <u>who</u> I'm walking with![107]

---

[107] Micah 6:8...what does the Lord require of you...but to walk humbly with Him?

Barefoot

I like the feel of a thick plush carpet of grass under my bare feet. I like dirt that is so soft and dry and fine that it feels like I am walking in talcum powder. I even like cool mud squished thickly between my toes on a hot summer day. And I like the way the Bible talks about feet.

Jesus, I think it is so sweet
That You washed the disciples feet.[108]

You did not wash their hands or faces
Or any less unpleasant places.

Mary used perfume, her tears and hair
To wash Your feet and show her care.[109]

Paul said, "How beautiful are the feet
Of those who preach the Gospel of Peace."[110]

God, You spoke from a bush to Moses[111]
And told him to expose his toes-es,

So, really it's not all that odd,
That barefoot, I feel close to God.

---

[108] John 13:5
[109] Luke 7:38
[110] Romans 10:15
[111] Exodus 3:4-5

70

Deby's Grandma

A lady died after suffering many years with Alzheimer's. I didn't know her. Her granddaughter was my friend, Deby. I went to the service because I was afraid there would be no one there to comfort my friend.

The family had done a collage of pictures of "Grandma" over the years. In almost every snapshot, she wore an old-fashioned bib apron with ruffles over the shoulders. The officiating pastor talked about how she had always been available for Sunday School, youth activities, Bible School and funeral dinners. She enjoyed cooking for any occasion.

I need not have worried about Deby going through the burial alone. I looked around at the people who remembered her Grandma and honored her that day. She had fed many of them one way or another. Pastor Jim held up one of those old aprons. "Folks," he said, "this was her armor in Christian service."

Afterward, I got to talk with the Pastor. I asked him if he would do my funeral service when I died. He said sure, if I'd do poetry at his. (We haven't worked the details out on that one yet.) "Jim," I said, "I don't really have any funeral poems." He said, "Oh, you'll think of something. Just start out with, 'Here he is dead in his boots.'"

Few poems are written off the cuff, but I think God had a hand in this one. It was written before I could drive the mile and a half home. Somewhere I still have the envelope that I jotted it down on.

 I called Pastor Jim's answering machine within minutes and left his poem there for him to find when he finished his Christian service that day.

71

Jim's Boots

Here he lies dead with his boots on
But in heaven, he'll no longer need 'em.

He'll dance before God just like David[112]
And those boots would only impede him.

So, yank off his boots: He's done working.
His labor on earth here is through.

But slip those boots onto your own feet:
There's plenty of work left for you!

---

[112] …David's wife got mad at him because of how he danced that day and if you don't know, II Samuel 6:14 is where you can check it out!

Footprints

"The Footprint Story"[113] tells about a person looking back across the sands of time and seeing two sets of footprints: God's and their own. At the toughest places in life, there is only one set of prints. The writer cries out at the injustice of being on his or her own at such times. God replies that no, it was at those times that He carried them.

My husband and I were discussing the footprint theory one day after he had received an e-mail about it. The conversation ended with my husband saying, "That ought to be a poem." And so it is:

When I get home to glory
And look back across sands of time

To see the footprint story
I know I'll see God's and mine

But I'm hoping too that I'll see
Where happiness was so real

That there are handprints in the sand
Where joy gave way to cartwheels!

---

[113] There is controversy about authorship of "The Foot Print Story." I am uncertain whom to credit.

Old Shoes

I love quotes. It's like getting to crawl into other peoples' heads and think their thoughts. C.S. Lewis, the man I knew first as the author of <u>The Lion, The Witch and The Wardrobe</u>, was also a deep thinker and theologian.

In <u>The Screwtape Letters</u>, he won my heart by saying, "It's so much easier to pray for a bore than to go and visit one." (It explained a lot to me about my lack of drop in company and why so many people that I haven't seen for a while will say to me, "Oh, I've been praying for you!")

Then, in <u>Letters to Malcolm</u>, C.S. Lewis wrote, "A good shoe is a shoe you don't notice." I believe this is a truth so compelling that it must have been inspired.

They aren't too loose.
They aren't too tight.
Old comfortable shoes hold your feet just right.

They don't rub or flop.
They don't draw attention.
Old comfortable shoes won't cause you tension.

The tongues of old shoes
Never complain.
The eyes of old shoes never view with disdain.

When I think of heaven
And going up there,
I dream of taking old shoes to wear!

Let
the
Son

Shine
in!

Spring Cleaning

I have a short attention span. Whereas I love the springtime, I still have a struggle because I lack that Dominant Good Housekeeping Gene.

It's springtime and I should be cleaning
But I stand at an open door

And gaze at what's green and growing
That I never noticed before.

You'd think that I'd be thankful
And sing praises to my Creator

But I just ♫stand amazed in the presence♫[114]

Of my refrigerator!

Lightning Bugs

Summertime is the season of porch-sitting, yard work and chatting with neighbors. It is also time for playing hide-and-seek in the dark. Once, we lost two children at this game. New neighbors had recently moved in. Our oldest daughter and a friend hid under their porch. The new folks came out to enjoy the evening. The kids were scared to come out till that went in. We were so relieved when the kids reappeared! I felt like the mother of the prodigal son.[115] Only I had a prodigal daughter!

Summertime is also firefly season. Faith is like a firefly... it shines best in the darkest times, it sheds a little light on gloomy situations and keeps you from being afraid.

Kids catch the living sparklers and bottle them up. The container of choice for making flickering lanterns used to be a glass Mason jar. Metal lids had air holes punched through with hammer and nail. They have now been replaced by safer, plastic peanut butter jars. Their bright colored lids have air holes drilled with cordless drills. We never wanted to 'waste' good bugs, so when our girls were "buggers," we encouraged release at bedtime. A few however were sacrificed to fashion. Their tails pinched off to make glowing jewelry.

God questioned Job about where he was when the morning stars sang together.[116] As I watch children chasing fireflies while stars dance overhead, I can almost hear the stars' song. In the dark and quiet of the night, when the sky seems to turn itself inside out and the stars seem close enough to touch, I marvel at the beauty, near and far.

---

[115] Luke 15:11-32
[116] Job 38:7

Star Light, Star Bright

God made the stars
To shine above
To wish on
Not to touch

But here below
Where we could reach

He gave us
Lightning bugs!

I like to think God sends along these "little lights" to bring us joy.[117] I sense His humor as I watch their taillights. How different society might be if He had installed such a glowing feature on us!

---

[117] 1st Timothy 6:17 says that God gives us all good things to enjoy!

Don't Waste It!

We had a trampoline in the backyard for years. The whole family (and sometimes extra kids) camped out on it on occasion. The best part was just lying there watching the stars freckle the face of the sky. We loved to watch for shooting stars. If we all happened to see the same one, it was double delight.

A twinkle.
A flick
Then gone so quick.

An eye-
Worthy sight.
Surely God's own delight.

A wink – its here.
A flash it's there.
A mystery beyond compare.

A clear night's
Respite.
Nature's glory in flight.

And the first one
You see's
Worth a wish if you please.

Catch it!

Puppy

Love

The Praising Pups

I am a light sleeper. I can recognize the howls, growls, barks and bays of most dogs in our neighborhood. When you live in town, that's simply a fact of life. (Of course, if you live in the country, there are the cows, crickets and coyotes...)

Once about 2:00a.m. I pounded on a neighbor's door to ask them to quiet their dogs. The dogs listened attentively and without so much as a whimper once their owner's lights came on. The neighbors were polite. I was ashamed. (We later moved away from that neighborhood.)

One night, the dogs were especially communicative. I did not go visit any neighbors. The sun was coming up. I was exhausted and discouraged. I opened the Bible to Luke 19 and read about Jesus' triumphal entry into Jerusalem. I got to that verse about how if the people were silent, the stones would cry out. "Ah ha," I thought, "Now I understand."

Last night,
The neighborhood dogs were barking
In joyful canine chorus,

As if the rocks and the mountains were not enough
And they were praising the Father for us.

So I am resolved to praise God more,
Every day to sing His glory,

So every night
*Those dogs will **not** be raising His praises for me!*

Now when I hear those dogs barking, it's like a private joke between God and me. I rouse and chuckle (and sometimes tell God I'll do better in the morning). I don't lose much sleep over those neighborhood "praise and worship" leaders!

Fat Old Dog

There are two opposing forces inside each of us[118] and I find sometimes I must walk away from a situation to figure out if I am operating on selfishness or righteousness. When the kids were teen-agers, they accused me of running away from home at such times! But, I often had to reset my inner compass. There is nothing like a long walk to help you find eternal perspective.

I often erroneously thought my way was the only way. I tried to qualify and quantify and control. As I look at my children now in young adulthood, I wish I had taken more walks back then. I might have saved us all some aggravation.

Today was nice for a walk.
Thought I'd hike around the block.

Relieve some tension, burn off some fat
And give the neighbor's dog a pat.

She's a fat old dog, all friendly and fine
Who lolls and basks in the warm sunshine.

She barks hello as my approach she hears.
She knows I'm a soft touch:
I'll scratch her ears.

---

[118] Romans 7:15 tells how Paul wanted to do some things and didn't (and vice versa) while Mark 14:38 says the spirit is willing but the flesh is weak

I thought to myself, "I know this dog well:
Every bark, howl and growl,
Every wag of the tail."

I thought that I knew her good-bye and hello.
(Which shows just how little
I really did know.)

For I didn't know yesterday
When we said good-bye
That it'd be the last for that dog and I:

Because I found out when I passed by today
That chain, house and dog dish,
They moved her away.

I'm hoping someday
I'll take a long jog
Down some other street
And I'll find that old dog

And maybe she'll bark
At the sound of my feet
And it'll be a reunion
Where two old friends meet.

The children grew up fine in spite of me and enough years have passed that I know that dog and I will not meet again. I should have taken more walks...

The

Financial

Pages

Find a Penny

"Find a penny pick it up, all day long you'll have good luck." When I learned that, I didn't know the difference between blessings and luck. I assumed both came from God.

For me, an unclaimed penny is like a little blessing, a sign that God was thinking about me.[119] Stray pennies are still like tangible reminders that Heaven is counting on me.

Find a penny.
Pick it up.
Toss it in the air.

If you catch it,
You will know
The reason it was there:
To remind you
God will find you
When you're lost or down,
And He will pick you up
And then
He'll turn your life around.
But if you drop that penny you toss
And worry God will drop you too
Just remember

♫He's got the whole world in His hands♫
And He still catches better than you!

---

[119] Last week, I found a dime while I was out walking with my husband. He asked if that meant God thought about me ten times, or did I owe God nine cents change. Go figure!

A Penny for your Thoughts

Folks used to say, "A penny for your thoughts." We have a good friend, Tony who likes to ask instead, "What's in your heart today?" It's hard to sidestep that question with trivialities.

I have come to realize that prayer is that same thing. It's what is in your heart today. It is simply not worrying about the formalities and communicating with God about what is happening in your life.

When you lose someone you love, there is no more opportunity for "penny talks." Your heart is full of leftover words and emotions. You can pour it all out to God. He understands. When my dad died, I wrote a request to God:

> *God, You took my earthly father home*
> *And left me feeling sad,*
> *So God my Father which art in heaven*
> *Would you say, "hi" to dad?*

Then Mother died. I reeled: I was an orphan. I wasn't anybody's little girl anymore. Nobody knew me like they did. Sure, I was old: I was forty-something, but I didn't have life all figured out yet. They weren't supposed to die till I was ready to take over my role as part of the older generation. God is gracious and good. He stayed with me as I stumbled through grief and transition.

Since I am now a part of the "old guard," I have stocked my penny supply. (Okay, I have also stocked a gumball machine so there is someplace to use those pennies!) And the neighbor kids come to visit. They come for the gumballs, but I try to remember to listen past the chomping…

A Penny on your Stone

I am learning that I cannot operate on "if only's." I am trying to learn from my losses and move on. This is especially true when someone I love dies. I get bogged down in all the regrets and good intentions. Cemeteries are great places for reflection…

Today I came to reminisce
To write my name in dust,
Below yours on the tombstone
That has separated us.

I live my life in retrospect
Here in the restless wind,
Remembering the happy times:
Living them again.

But I recall some bad times, too,
With sorrow and regret
For things I didn't know back then
And some I'll never get.

I can't change a one of them
But lately I'm coming to see
I'm learning still from all those things
And they are changing me.

So before I go I lay a shining
Penny on your stone:

A penny for the thoughts I think
When we are here alone.

Bon Appetite

Well, that's enough of my Baloney. I pray that every day your life will be sandwiched in the Living Bread...

Remember, Emmanuel is God with us[120]...covering us, wrapping His love around our lives. God wants to be with you. You don't have to know a lot of high-sounding words or churchy phrases. You just welcome Him into your life. He wants you...that is why He sent His Son as your Redeemer (and mine). I have a lot to learn, a lot of spiritual lunches to eat yet, and I hope to share more with you another time.

Meanwhile, may His reassuring love and tender care make your life tasty and easy to swallow!

Blessings on your Head!

Life is good,

Gayle Morris

---

[120] Matthew 1:23